The truth in their

He stinks of sweat!

She wears too much
perfume! Phew!

find out what
11- to 14-year-olds **REALLY**
think about each other...

www.**kidsatrandomhouse**.co.uk

IT'S A BOY/GIRL THING
A Red Fox Book 0 09 943212 9

First published in Great Britain by Red Fox,
an imprint of Random House Children's Books

Red Fox edition published 2003

1 3 5 7 9 10 8 6 4 2

Papers used by Random House Children's Books are natural, recyclable products
made from wood grown in sustainable forests.
The manufacturing processes conform to the environmental
regulations of the country of origin.

Set in 12/16 Toddler

Red Fox Books are published by Random House Children's Books,
61–63 Uxbridge Road, London W5 5SA,
a division of The Random House Group Ltd,
in Australia by Random House Australia (Pty) Ltd,
20 Alfred Street, Milsons Point, Sydney, NSW 2061, Australia,
in New Zealand by Random House New Zealand Ltd,
18 Poland Road, Glenfield, Auckland 10, New Zealand,
and in South Africa by Random House (Pty) Ltd,
Endulini, 5A Jubilee Road, Parktown 2193, South Africa.

THE RANDOM HOUSE GROUP Limited Reg. No. 954009
www.kidsatrandomhouse.co.uk

A CIP catalogue for this book is available from the British Library.

Printed and bound in Great Britain by
Bookmarque Ltd, Croydon, Surrey

It's A BOY GIRL Thing!

compiled by
Anne Finnis & Denis Bond

RED FOX

abc 296/2

contents

bleeep!
bleeep!

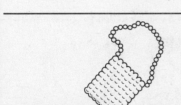

bleeep!
bleeep!

Have you ever wondered what **BOYS** and **GIRLS** **really** think about each other? Do you sometimes feel that members of the **opposite sex** are so weird they must come from another planet? Knowing what **they think** might just make a difference...

Over a hundred **boys** and a hundred **girls** from all over Britain were asked what they thought about the opposite sex. **It's A Boy/Girl Thing** is packed full of their opinions.

Of course everybody is different and many of the statements conflict with one another. While several of the girls hated boys' **hairy legs**, lots of others thought they were **sexy**.

While most of the boys liked girls with **long hair**, some said they hated long hair because it was always getting in the way.

This book tries to show a range of all the thoughts and opinions expressed. Some of these will make you **laugh out loud**, some are brilliantly observed and some will make you so **angry** you'll want to throw the book at the wall.

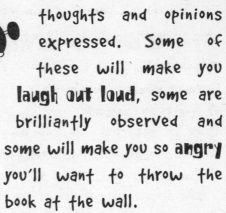

So, are members of the **opposite sex** really an **alien species**? Or are they just like **you** underneath? Here's your chance to find out...

bleeep!
bleeep!

What makes a BOY cool?

✿ **THEY'VE GOT TO SMELL NICE - NO SWEATY BITS.**

✿ Being clean, every hair in place, dressed well, taller than me, nice looking.

✿ If they play football.

✿ He has to be rich - to spend money on me.

✿ They need to wear the latest fashion.

✿ Someone who understands you - who's sensitive. Someone who doesn't mess around all the time, who listens to you, as well as jokes with you.

✿ A boy boy. Someone who can defend himself.

✿ Someone who's sophisticated.

What makes a GIRL cool?

★ **THE WAY SHE ACTS . . . BODY LANGUAGE.**

★ Good looks, personality, hairstyle, nice body and decent-sized boobies!

★ If she has money - so she can spend it on us.

★ The way they walk.

* The way she looks at you.
* She's got to wear the latest designer clothes, with lots of jewellery and big earrings.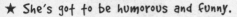
* She's got to be humorous and funny.
* She's got to be someone who would stick by me.
* She's not too worried about her looks and she wouldn't mind if she broke a nail.

How do BOYS dress?

✿ **SOME DRESS TO IMPRESS, BUT THEY TRY TOO HARD.**
✿ They wear stuff that doesn't match – navy and black.
✿ They haven't got any dress sense. Girls know what's fashionable. Boys all look the same.
✿ Some of them put on the first thing they see in the wardrobe.

 ## How do GIRLS dress?

★ **CLOTHES MATTER TO GIRLS A LOT MORE.**
★ Girls dress to impress. They dress up more than boys. Boys just put on their old clothes to play football, but when the girls come out they're in new croptops and tight trousers.
★ They spend ages getting ready. They've got to have the right earrings in and piles of rings on. They spray themselves with all stuff.

★ They spend a lot more money than boys on clothes.
And they can't live without their make-up.

What do BOYS eat?

✿ JUNK FOOD!
✿ Chips and burgers.
Sausage and chips.
Chips with everything.
✿ They never eat Polos
because they think it kills their sperm. They believe it!

- That weird raw egg drink: they put egg in a blender with salt and some fibre-pill thing and mix it up. They think it's going to make the muscles in their stomach tighten and go in.
- Anything that's not healthy – chocolate cake, pizza and ice cream. A big massive fry-up at the weekends.
- Anything they can find in the fridge or on the table.
- They don't eat salad because it's healthy and because they'd be considered a wuss.

What do GIRLS eat?

★ **A GRAPE – BECAUSE IT'S HEALTHY.**

★ Nothing. They don't like eating anything because they want to stay thin. They think it makes them look better. Or they eat it and then throw up.

★ 70% of girls don't eat breakfast. They want to be thin – it's sad.

★ They'll have nothing for breakfast, but they'll eat chocolate at break.

★ More girls are vegetarian than boys, because they don't like eating fluffy little animals.

★ They won't eat burgers because they're all greasy.

★ A Mars bar or a salad sandwich because it's cheap.

★ They don't want to eat meat because they don't like to see animals with their heads sliced off.

★ Girls drink water instead of Coke – because it's healthier. They have a bottle of water in their bag so they can drink it in the lesson. They want to flush their systems to make their waste go away, so they don't get fat, and so they don't burp and fart.

How are BOYS different to GIRLS (apart from the obvious)?

✿ **THEY USE MORE SLANG. THEY'RE COCKY. LOUDER.**

✿ Most boys spend hours in the bathroom every morning spiking their hair up with loads of gel. People say girls take longer over their appearance, but I doubt it.

✿ When they walk they sway, their shoulders swing, their arms are out so they look like they've got rolls of carpet under them.

How are GIRLS different to BOYS (apart from the obvious)?

★ **GIRLS DO THEIR HAIR ALL THE TIME.**

★ They all have these big brushes.

★ Some girls are bossy in the way they speak. They want to get their own way.

★ They don't speak as quick – they explain things.

★ They have more stuff to say than boys.

★ They speak posher than boys.

★ Their bodies are pear-shaped. Their hips go funny, they're bigger, wider. It's for having babies.

Are BOYS more mature than GIRLS?

✿ **THEY'RE IMMATURE. THEY MAKE FUN OF THEIR FRIENDS IN FRONT OF THEM AND THEY TELL EVERYONE EACH OTHER'S SECRETS.**

✿ They try and embarrass their mates to make themselves look good.

✿ Boys dress up to look older – it doesn't work . . .

✿ All boys care about is girls, all they care about is girls and football, all they care about is girls, football and dirty films, all they care about is girls, football, dirty films and alcohol.

Are GIRLS more mature than BOYS?

★ **GIRLS TRY TO BE MORE GROWN UP.**

★ Girls worry about things that don't really matter like their hair and their nails.

★ Girls are more mature about work, but when it comes to stuff like parties they go all immature.

★ Most girls are childish. They talk in weird giggly, squeaky voices. They stick their hands over their mouths and whisper.

★ They're always sending notes
   around the class.

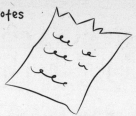

Are BOYS different in the way
they express their emotions?

✿ **GIRLS TALK ABOUT THINGS - BOYS KEEP THINGS INSIDE.**
✿ Boys can be sensitive - they are affected by things
   that happen like the death of somebody close just as
   much as girls.
✿ They think it's uncool to show their emotions. But it's good
   when they show their more feminine side.
✿ Boys are more romantic than girls.

 Are GIRLS different in the way
they express their emotions?

★ **GIRLS AREN'T SCARED TO TELL PEOPLE
   HOW THEY FEEL.**
★ Even if they only saw each other ten minutes ago,
   girls give each other a big hug.
★ If one starts crying, they all start crying - it's like
   a chain reaction. It's like a Mexican wave of hugs
   and tears.

Are BOYS more intelligent than GIRLS?

✿ **No!!! BOYS ACT BRAIN DEAD.**

✿ Boys' brains are divided into two halves – half for sex and half for food.

✿ They might be more intelligent but they don't want to show it because everyone would say they're such a boffin. So they act like they're really dumb.

✿ Some people say boys have got bigger brains. If they **HAVE** got bigger brains they waste them too much on sex.

✿ The 'bigger brain' thing shows how stupid they are! It's not the **SIZE** of your brain that matters!

✿ Boys and girls have got about the same intelligence – but boys don't revise and they get bad marks. They don't read the questions because they think they know it all, and they don't concentrate.

✿ Boys think they're hard and they laugh if they get zero in tests.

✿ Boys are more intelligent than girls. And they're more big-headed.

> They've got a brain. They just don't use it!

Are GIRLS more intelligent than BOYS?

★ **THEY <u>THINK</u> THEY ARE.**

★ Girls try harder than the boys.

★ They are kind of brainier than us, because they don't muck around.

★ Girls are more intelligent – except for blondes. Then they're bimbos.

★ Girls are more swotty. They like to study a lot.

★ No, they just use their brain because they **WANT** to use it.

★ It's been proven that girls are smarter than boys, but I don't think it's right. They just prefer to get on more in their work; boys prefer to play football and sports.

★ Some girls are really stupid. When you talk about something they come out with stupid things.

★ Girls are more intelligent because if a teacher asks you a question and you don't know the girls will tell you.

★ They revise for a test, we don't. We'd probably achieve the same if we revised.

★ A boy's brain has larger parts concentrating on sex. Girls have a larger part that says shopping.

What subjects do BOYS prefer?

❀ **BOYS LIKE SEX EDUCATION . . .**

❀ Boys like the laid-back lessons where they don't have to do much work.

❀ They like PE and sport because they're competing against each other and they can show off their skills.

❀ PE because they can muck about and it's physical and they don't have to be writing and reading.

❀ They like science so they can mess around with chemicals.

❀ Art: boys like to draw little cartoon characters and because they like to graff.

❀ IT - to go on the Net.

What subjects do GIRLS prefer?

★ **GIRLS LOVE SITTING DOWN ALL DAY AND WRITING.**

★ Creative subjects: art, textiles and cooking.

★ They don't like maths 'cos they have to work too hard.

★ They like subjects where they don't get messy - English, history, humanities.

★ They love to show off their neat handwriting. They have all these flash pens with different colours and scents.

★ They prefer sewing and food tech. So they can be the perfect little housewives - because they belong in the kitchen.

★ Girls complain that they get splinters in their fingers in DT.

★ They squirm about dissecting things. They don't like practical stuff.

Do BOYS care about dieting and exercise?

✿ **BOYS GO TO THE GYM - TO GET A SIX-PACK.**

✿ If you say to them you're getting a bit chubby they'll go straight to the gym. They're not bothered about actual dieting or food, but they're worried about how they look.

✿ They'd rather be fit than flabby. They're concerned about their bodies because they want to impress the girls.

✿ Some of them get fit without knowing it, 'cos they're always on their bikes, playing football or chasing after the girls.

✿ Boys go straight for the weights. They put on about six weights . . . and can't move it!

✿ Some go to the gym to work on their pecs. Every time they're out it's 'feel that, feel that' – the muscles in their arms.

Do GIRLS care about dieting and exercise?

★ **THEY'RE ALWAYS ON DIETS.**

★ It's more not eating really. They wouldn't get up and run round the block. They're too lazy.

★ They're afraid of being fat, but they don't do any exercise, they're too afraid of breaking their nails.

★ Girls who are quite fat say they never eat, then you see them eating all the time!

★ They always seem to have a massive arse – food goes to their arses.

★ They do aerobics to get their legs nice to get the boys. They go to the gym to strengthen their tummy muscles – to show off to the boys.

★ The only exercise their arms get is holding their umbrellas.
   But they've still got fat arms.
★ They do weight-lifting with their shopping bags.

★ They exercise their arms by doing their hair.
★ The only exercise they do is walking around the shops.

Girls think they're fat when they're not. They're paranoid!

Imagine a BOY'S bedroom...

✿ **IT STINKS OF SWEATY SOCKS AND B.O.**

✿ They don't open the curtains, they don't make the bed, they can't be bothered - they expect their mum to make it.

✿ They don't open the windows. There are dirty clothes everywhere, they leave left-over food in their room - and the smell!

What's on the wall?

✿ **NO SMOKING SIGNS, ROAD SIGNS AND TROPHIES.**

✿ Posters of football teams, wrestlers, WWF women, half-naked women, skateboarders, girls they like from the telly and computer games, cars, motorbikes, pop stars, rock bands, rap, heavy metal stars, garage and hip-hop stars.

What's on the bed?

* ✿ **DIRTY PLATES AND STUFF. HARD PIZZA.**
* ✿ The duvet is a mess, crumpled up in a pile or half hanging off the bed, with clothes, dirty underwear, sweaty socks, homework, CDs and magazines just chucked all over.

* ✿ All boys have rolled-up pieces of tissue.
* ✿ The teddy that nobody knows about.
* ✿ He'd only have pencils and books if he was a nerd.
* ✿ A wet patch in the morning.
* ✿ Condom packets purposely – to make you think he knows what he's doing.

What's under the bed?

* ✿ **TORTURED TEDDIES AND PANTS WITH SKID MARKS.**
* ✿ They'll have a secret stash of porn mags and porn videos.
* ✿ If they say they're going to tidy their room it only takes a minute because they shove everything under the bed. So there's rubbish, crisp packets, sweet wrappers, old toys and dirty clothes that have been there for months.
* ✿ There's always a half-eaten sandwich under the bed because they get someone to make it for them, then they get a phone call – somebody wants them to play football, they say, 'Yeah,' and walk out.

✿ The Daily Sport and cuttings of Page Three Girls.

✿ Plates with mouldy food on them, old cups of tea, empty Nutella jars and spoons and yoghurt pots that have gone slimy.

What's hidden in his secret drawer?

✿ **THE LOVEY-DOVEY STUPID STUFF.**

✿ Normal stuff on the top – underneath money that he's nicked from his parents, magazines he's not allowed to have, food – chocolate bars, eighteen-rated videos.

✿ They would probably have a picture of someone they fancied and they'd kiss it before they go to bed.

✿ Lists of people they fancy that they don't want anybody to know about. Like, if he fancies a boffin, or another boy, or someone his friends had been insulting. He'd never tell anybody.

✿ A list of the best websites to find naked girls on.

✿ Women's underwear because it turns them on.

✿ Some of the lads might have drugs – cannabis (dope, weed, bong).

- ✿ Condoms - they're interested to see what they're like.
- ✿ Empty beer cans. Bottles of alcohol.
- ✿ Knives - they tattoo themselves with knives and compasses. Cigarettes and lighters.
- ✿ Love letters. If they get love letters in front of their mates they pretend they're not bothered, but they take them home and keep them.

 Imagine a GIRL'S bedroom...

★ **PINK AND FLOWERY.**

★ There'll be a messy dressing table covered with make-up boxes and brushes. It stinks of perfume. There'll be a big stereo and there's CDs scattered on the floor with the thongs. It's tidier than a boy's room though.

What's on the wall?

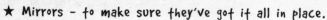

★ **MASSIVE SHELVES OF MAKE-UP.**

★ Posters of boy bands, soap and movie stars, footballers. Pictures of muscly guys or pop stars with no tops on, because they like their bodies.

★ Mirrors - to make sure they've got it all in place.

★ Teddy bears and china dolls on shelves. Books. Awards - for things like horse-riding.

★ Pictures of somebody they love - either somebody famous or their boyfriend.

★ Class photos with rings around people they like, and photos of their friends.

What's on the bed?

★ **LOADS OF DIFFERENT KINDS OF TEDDY BEARS.**

★ A white and pink duvet and a big heart-shaped frilly pink pillow.

★ Clothes, bras and knickers from the day before and a nightdress - red and short.

★ There's a picture of someone they love under their pillow.
★ Their favourite agony aunt's magazines.

What's under the bed?

★ **STUFF THEY WANT TO HIDE.**
★ Designer shoes that they only wore yesterday, but girls think they're old because they've worn them once.
★ Clothes, either because they need washing and she can't be bothered to do it, or they're expensive and her mum doesn't know about them and she'll be cross. Or she smokes – and the smell is on the clothes so she's hiding them.
★ Everything that's not cool, like old Barbie dolls and things from when they were younger.
★ Biscuit crumbs, toenail clippings, sweets. All the mess she's swept up.
★ They'll hide their diary under the bed if Mum knocks on the door.
★ Pictures of old boyfriends. Teddy bears that were given to them by boyfriends they've been dumped by, so the teddy's been ripped.
★ Condoms. Dirty magazines and dirty toys.

What's hidden in her secret drawer?

★ **LOVE LETTERS.**

★ A diary. Every girl has a personal diary with secret stuff in about who they love, what they've done with them, who they fancy.

★ There'll be fags, lighters and spirits. Expensive jewellery from an older boyfriend.

★ There might be some drugs – cannabis.

★ Sanitary towels and tampons that she wants to hide.

★ Photos of her boyfriend, or ex-boyfriends, or boys she fancies.

★ A piece of hair from a boy she's fancied.

★ condoms, special clothes that make them look dead sexy, but are secret so their mum doesn't find them, sentimental pictures, pregnancy pills and pregnancy tests.

★ Pictures of nude boys.

★ A secret wad of money so they can go shopping.

★ Love letters – the ones they've written but never had the guts to send.

★ Thongs to impress the boys. They wear their trousers low, and pull them up high.

★ Pictures of them and their friends taken in photo booths. They keep them in their purse too.

What do BOYS do in their free time?

✿ **THEY WATCH FOOTIE.**
✿ Boys watch TV and eat.

✿ They play fighting games on the computer
✿ They go online – visiting porn websites and chatlines.
✿ They look at dirty magazines and do rude things with themselves.

What do GIRLS do in their free time?

★ **THEY TRY DIFFERENT MAKE-UP AND HAIR DOS.**
★ They invite their boyfriends over, or phone their boyfriends.

★ While a girl's on the phone she's looking in the mirror, changing her clothes and talking.

★ They're always talking to friends on the phone, even if her friend lives next door! They're reading magazines, listening to music, watching TV, washing their hair.

Do BOYS get on better with their mums or their dads?

✿ HE'LL BE LOVING WITH HIS MUM. MORE HARD WITH HIS DAD.

✿ He'll like his mum for buying him stuff like pants and pyjamas and because he can tell her things like who he fancies. He'll like his dad for taking him out to football matches and being a man.

✿ Some boys are scared of their dads, but they'll be cheeky to their mums.

✿ They don't like their dad – he tells them what to do.

✿ They're closer to their mums because mums have no idea what boys are really like or what they're getting up to. Mums think their boys are little angels.

✿ If you cuss a boy's mum he'll start fighting. But if you say anything against his dad he's like, 'Yeah, so what about my dad?'

✿ He's closer to his dad – he might think his mum's embarrassing.

✿ His dad is most like him and gives him advice because dads know what boys get up to. Dads know what really goes on because they were doing it at their age.

✿ They spend more time with their dads – they go to football matches, play sport and go fishing with them.

✿ They share their dirty habits – they belch and burp together and laugh at each other.

Do GIRLS get on better with their mums or their dads?

★ **THEIR MUM BECAUSE THEY CAN TALK TO HER ABOUT THEIR GIRLIE PROBLEMS.**

★ When they're younger they like their dads more, but as they get older they get embarrassed by their dads.

★ Mums are usually softer. They can wrap Mum round their little finger, they'll start being nice and do the housework so then they get to go to town with their friends.

★ Mum, because they can share their secrets and she gives them advice on shopping and boys and make-up and hair.

★ They get on better with their dads - it's always daddy's little girl. Dads are the gullible ones; she can sweet-talk her dad.

★ Dad because he's got the money. They whine and whinge at him until they get some.

★ Dads worry about girls going out with older lads - they'll worry about sex, drugs, that sort of thing. They understand what the boys will be doing because that's what they did.

★ They get told by their dads, they argue with their mums.

What jobs do BOYS do around the house?

✿ **THEY DON'T EVEN PUT THEIR UNDERWEAR IN THE WASHING BASKET.**

✿ They should be expected to do everything the girls are expected to do, but they're not.

✿ Boys are sexist. They think it's the girls who should be doing it all. They won't do anything unless they've been told to.

✿ They say things like, 'I've got to wipe the table, which cloth shall I use?' When you say, 'I dunno,' they'll say, 'You're the woman, you should know.'

✿ They don't iron, wash up or cook.

✿ Some can cook. They can do curries and things like that. They learn how to make toast and an egg or something at school.

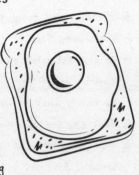

✿ They expect their mums to do it. Boys rely on their mums.

✿ They say that men should be equal to women and women equal to men but they don't do anything – they expect the women to do it all.

✿ Boys get so used to having things done for them that they wouldn't think of doing it for themselves.

Do BOYS expect to get paid?

❀ **BOYS EXPECT A FIVER TO DO THEIR ROOM.**

❀ Yes. They think if they've got to do a woman's job they've got to be paid.

❀ They want to know what they're going to get. They only do stuff if they have a reason.

❀ If they want a game or something, they'll say they'll only do the washing up if you get me it.

What jobs do GIRLS do around the house?

★ **GIRLS ARE SLAVES.**

★ Girls make tea.

★ Cleaning and cooking is a woman's job - that's what they were born for.

★ It's a girl's job to do the cooking. It's not a manly thing, cooking, is it? Boys can't cook. We rely more on snacks. Boys shouldn't have to do it. Girls **LIKE** doing it.

★ They can't cook - boys do it better.

★ The cleaning, the washing, cooking, doing the dishes, the ironing. Boys are not supposed to iron. It's a girl thing.

★ Girls should do more than boys - it's what they're there for. Girls are multi-tasked.

★ I think the girls are going to stop slaving around after men, because of women's rights and all that.

★ They're more dainty, so they do more dainty jobs around the house like dusting. They don't want to do things in the garden because it'll break their nails.

★ Girls want to tidy up their bedrooms, especially if their boyfriend is coming round.

★ Girls have to do their own washing and ironing because they've got so many clothes their parents refuse to do it.

Do GIRLS expect to get paid?

★ **YES. GIRLS WANT MORE MONEY FOR CLOTHES, MAKE-UP, SHOES, UNDERWEAR...**

★ No, because when they grow up and get married they'll be expected to do all the housework. 'Cos if the bloke goes out to work and gets all the money – the girl does the housework at home.

★ No. They do it to get on their mum's side. They do it for respect and because they want things to be pretty and nice.

★ They don't expect to be paid like the boys, but they will expect their parents to allow them out an hour later in the evening.

What sort of pet would a BOY have?

✿ **BOYS LIKE DOGS BECAUSE THEY'RE BOTH MAD!**

✿ They'd like a pet that doesn't take much looking after or one that scares people like spiders, reptiles, snakes, rats or ferrets.

✿ A big vicious dog because they can threaten you with them – 'I'll get my dog on you.' You can't say, 'I'll get my rabbit on you.'

✿ It's got to be a hard dog like a bulldog because it looks scary and so it makes them look tough.

✿ A Dobermann, Rottweiler, or Staff – hard dogs. They think it makes them look all hard, but really you're laughing.

✿ If anyone bought them a poodle they'd hate it because it looks girlie.

✿ To impress a girl they might get a fluffy kitten.

What sort of pet would a GIRL have?

★ **GIRLS WANT CUTE PETS SO THEY CAN HUG THEM - YOU CAN'T HUG A FISH.**

★ A cute fluffy thing like a hamster, rabbit, cat. They'll get compliments from their friends.

★ A cat - all cuddly and fluffy. They can snuggle up to it.

★ A hamster because it's small, girly and cute.

★ A cat because they like furry stuff. They can stroke it and make a fuss of it and talk to it and tell it all their problems. A hamster would chew their nails for them if they got too long.

★ A rabbit so they can brush its hair.

★ They like ponies. It gives them something to do, like clean them out in their spare time.

A boy, because they reckon they can treat him like a pet and do whatever they like with him. But they can't.

How would BOYS treat a pet?

✿ **THEY'D USE IT TO SHOW OFF.**

✿ They'd take it to school and scare all the girls.

✿ He'd spoil it. He'd treat it like his brother.

✿ They can't be arsed to do anything with it. They'd shove the food in the bowl and leave it. They'd get their mum to clean up after it.

✿ They take it for a walk, but actually the dog is taking them for a walk.

✿ Boys are evil to animals. I've seen them setting them alight and putting them in microwaves.

✿ They'd look after it, but they wouldn't fuss over it. I think they'd train it to bite people or to chase them.

How would GIRLS treat a pet?

★ **THEY'D TREAT IT LIKE A BEST FRIEND.**

★ They'll be really kind to it. Give it treats, and they'd buy it everything.

★ They'll be combing the rabbit to make it look nice, like them.

Even if it was bad they'd still say, 'oh, who's a good boy!'

★ They'd look after it for about a week and then they'd forget about it. They wouldn't bother about it until someone said, 'It's dying,' and then they'd say, 'ooh, I love it so much.'

★ Even if it was a boy they'd put bows in its hair.

that's life
...at school

bleeep!
bleeep!

What do BOYS think about school?

❀ **BOYS HATE SCHOOL.**

❀ They don't really care.

❀ They can't be bothered.

❀ They hang around the toilets. They walk in late whenever they want. They're always fighting and they bang on the windows.

What do GIRLS think about school?

★ **THEY ARE GOODY-GOODIES, TEACHER'S PETS.**

★ Girls want to be at school so they can learn more. They're more swotty.

★ They've always got their hands up. They answer all the questions.

★ They've always got the equipment they need: pens, rulers and stuff. It's all neat.

What are BOYS like in the classroom?

✿ **BOYS ARE ALWAYS TRYING TO BE CLASS CLOWNS.**
✿ They show off to try to make the girls laugh.
✿ They take the mickey out of things you say.
✿ There's two types of boys: there's the boffs who just sit in the corner working all the time and then there's the ones who shout at the teacher and won't do any work. They want to be the centre of attention.
✿ They always swing on chairs and bang on desks.
✿ They chuck rubbers about and they put tacks on people's seats.
✿ They try to act hard in front of their mates. They're trying to impress each other and the girls.

What are GIRLS like in the classroom?

★ **THEY'RE REALLY LOUD AND THEY GIGGLE A LOT.**
★ They work! You're trying to talk to them and they want to get on.
★ Girls just gossip at the back of the room. Somehow they manage to have a full conversation and still be working!
★ They never stop chatting. They whisper about boys.

★ They send notes around the classroom, normally about a boy they like, but when the boy finds out they get all embarrassed and say, 'I didn't write it, I didn't write it.'
★ They all stick up for each other.
★ They like to be in charge a lot. They're chatty, but when they get caught they say it's the lads.
★ Some are really flirty – they lean over to make sure you can see their breasts.

What about BOYS' attitude to teachers?

✿ **BOYS WIND THE TEACHERS UP ALL THE TIME.**

✿ They're all cocky. They pretend they don't care: 'oh, so what, it's a teacher.'

✿ Some of the boys are too scared to answer back.

✿ They argue with the teachers. They talk back.

✿ They're really cheeky. They've got an attitude problem. Then, when the teacher says, 'What's wrong?' they grunt, 'Uh, uh, nothing.'

✿ They make silly noises like farts. Sometimes they do it for real. Sometimes they make duck noises and cat noises to irritate everyone.

✿ Boys always try and get a bad reputation. They want the teacher to shout at them so they can tell their friends, 'I was bad today in class.'

What about GIRLS' attitude to teachers?

★ **THEY FLIRT WITH THE TEACHER.**

★ They feel they're on the same wavelength as teachers because they think they're more mature.

★ They say they like this teacher but when they're out of the classroom they'll say, 'I hate this teacher. I could have slapped her' – things like that.

★ A bit cocky. Girls are ready for an argument.

★ They're good all the time. They act very posh. They sit straight. They're courteous, they're always sucking up to the teachers.

★ The teachers don't tell the girls off – never.

★ They put on a sweet voice when they're talking: 'Can you help me, sir?' They're always trying to soft up the teachers.

How do BOYS behave in the playground?

✿ **THEY'D DO ANYTHING TO GET YOU BEHIND THE BIKE SHEDS.**

✿ Boys mess around more.

✿ They fight a lot. Girls fight too, but girls are verbal, boys are physical.

✿ They kick over the dustbins – every time we come to school there's rubbish everywhere; the playground is always messy because of them.

✿ They think they're really good for putting litter in girls' hair and stuff like that.

✿ They have their sidekick standing there just to make sure that someone will laugh at them, even if they're not funny.

✿ They call girls stupid names. They lift our skirts up.

✿ They say things to you like, 'Let me give you a kiss . . .' and dirty things.

✿ They try and sweet-talk you. They say things like, 'You're a very pretty lady.' They charm you.

✿ They're prats. They're always showing off. They act as if they own the place.

✿ They come and annoy you: they hit you or pull the bobble out of your hair. They're just trying to get attention.

 How do GIRLS behave in the playground?

★ **GIRLS JUST SIT AROUND AND GOSSIP.**

★ They're in the smokers' corner.

★ They try and take the ball when we're playing football.

★ They get a friend to come over and say they fancy you.

★ They like to be the rulers and order people to do things.

★ If they don't like you or you're not as high up in the
populars as they are, they'll call you names and say they
want to go out with you. Then they say, 'oh, no, I was
only joking. You're just an idiot anyway.'

★ They go around in a massive group of friends.

★ The girls slag boys off.

★ They do you over and that. If you annoy
them they hit you or slap you.

★ They run over and spray you with stuff
like Impulse.

★ They huddle in their group, and
they stand in a sexy way to attract
the boys.

★ They look at you and talk about you but you don't know
what about.

★ They start to flirt with the boys.

★ They come up and try to cuddle you.

★ If one of them was crying they
all huddle round and cuddle
them and talk to them.

★ You can never get girls on their
own; they always hang around
in gangs.

★ They talk about their hair.
They're always complimenting
each other.

★ They bitch about other girls.

★ They laugh when somebody trips over.

★ If you're normal then it's all right, but if you're not they
pick on you.

How do BOYS respond to discipline?

✿ **THEY THINK IT'S COOL TO GET INTO TROUBLE. IF THEY DO GET INTO TROUBLE THEY DON'T TELL THEIR MUMS AND DADS.**

✿ They're like, 'What have I done?' They pretend they don't know what they've done.

✿ They run around the school doing what they want. They think they own the school.

✿ If they get told off they just laugh. They pretend they don't care but they really do.

✿ They like to say how many sanctions they've got.

How do GIRLS respond to discipline?

★ **THEY SAY, 'IT WASN'T ME, IT WAS HIM OR HER.'**

★ Girls hate being told off. They can't take it. They get in a right stress.

★ If they get told off they put on puppy eyes or turn on the water works. They twirl their hair.

★ They say it's unfair and they hold a grudge against the teacher that told them off.

How about BOYS' attitude to homework?

✿ **THEY THINK IT'S COOL NOT TO DO HOMEWORK.**
✿ They never ever do it. They just laugh.
✿ Some boys say they didn't do their homework and are all mouthy about it. Then they give it in without saying a word.
✿ Boys do it all scruffy because they can't write properly.
✿ Most boys do it in class before the start of the lesson.
✿ They call girls swots for doing their homework.
✿ They try to get girls to do their homework.
✿ They don't do it; going out is more important.

How about GIRLS' attitude to homework?

★ **THEY ACTUALLY DO IT!**
★ They always do their homework even if they copy.
★ It's always really neat, but they say it's scruffy.
★ They pretend it's really hard then hand it in early.
★ Girls do homework because they're boffs and teacher's pets.

★ They have to colour everything in.

★ It's always in on time.

★ It's always nicely presented. They put their best efforts into it. Girls bring these big plastic packages, boys just put it in their homework folder.

What about BOYS' attitude to tests?

✿ **THEY LIE ABOUT WHAT GRADE THEY GET.**

✿ They brag about not revising. It's cool not to do it. When they get a bad result they think it's really good.

✿ They say they're really easy.

✿ They say they only got a low mark because they didn't work.

✿ They say they don't revise because they think they'll get picked on if they do.

✿ They say, 'I don't care.' They're not going to work when they get older because they think they're going to be footballers.

✿ They just look at your test and copy from you.

✿ Boys get all jealous because teachers say the girls are better.

✿ They don't revise – they're outside playing or chilling with their friends.

✿ Behind all their porno magazines they've really got their mathematics books.

What about GIRLS' attitude to tests?

★ **GIRLS REALLY REALLY CARE ABOUT THE STUPID TESTS.**

★ They try to be rebels by saying they didn't revise. Then they do really well.

★ They cry a lot around SATS.

★ A little test next day, and they'll spend all night revising.

★ They say they've got to revise, they stay in and do it.

★ Girls are worried about the future. They think what will I do when I'm older? A boy thinks, Live life now – enjoy it.

★ They always try to revise hard so they don't get bad marks, so the boys will go after them.

Do BOYS get to school on time?

✿ **BOYS ARE ALWAYS LATE BECAUSE THEY MESS ABOUT.**

✿ They're usually on time so they can eat all the food from the canteen.

✿ They're always late because they go to the shop on the way to school to get something to eat or they forget something and go back for it.

✿ They stay up too late so they always sleep in.

✿ They're messing around at home with things like their GameBoys so then they're late.

✿ If it's PE or something they like they're always on time; if it's something like English or languages they're late.

Do GIRLS get to school on time?

★ **GIRLS COME IN EARLY FOR A MORNING CHAT.**

★ Girls are late because they're concentrating on how they look and doing their hair – hair is the main factor.

★ They lie in, then, at the last minute, get up and do their make-up. They spend ages getting sorted.

★ They do their make-up while they're walking!

★ They get up about five hours earlier than us to do their hair and make-up. They put about three coats of foundation and blusher on.

★ They're usually tired all day because they got up early to do their hair.

Do BOYS play truant (bunk, skive, wag it, whack it)?

✿ **BOYS SKIVE ALL THE TIME.**

✿ A lot say they're going to bunk off and then you see them sitting in class.

✿ One says, 'I'll do it if **YOU** do it,' and the other one says, 'I'll do it if **YOU** do it . . .' and they don't!

✿ Some of them pretend that they do – they say they've wagged it loads of times to get in with the popular people.

✿ For boys it's a game. They run around school and they'll hide when a teacher comes.

✿ They might tell their mums they're ill and stay at home, then they say they weren't away ill, they were bunking off. And sometimes they say they've been bunking off, but really they've been sick.

 # And where do they go?

✿ **THEY GO TO THE TOILETS.**

✿ They skive in the trees and bushes – messing around, fighting, having a laugh.

✿ They go to the shops, or McDonald's.

✿ They're likely to stay at home because they're too scared to go anywhere else.

* They stand in 'fag alley' and smoke.
* They go to the park – no one can see them there. They climb trees, smoke, act hard, eat and fart.
* They might go nicking up in town – from sweet shops or from bike shops.

Do GIRLS play truant (bunk, skive, wag it, whack it)?

★ **GIRLS DON'T SKIVE.**
★ They brag about skiving, but if they get caught they blame one of the boys.
★ They do a lap round the corridor so they're two minutes late and say they've been skiving.

And where do they go?

★ **TO THEIR BOYFRIEND'S HOUSE.**
★ To the shopping centre – to shop. They never stop. They need something new all the time.

★ They go down town to see the older lads that have already left school.
★ They say they went to the shops, but then you find out they've just been sitting at home.
★ They go somewhere where the police won't find them.
★ They go and have a fag in the alleys or in the bushes.

abc   296/2
time out

bleeep!
bleeep!

What sort of entertainment do BOYS like?

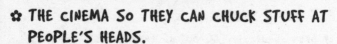

✿ **THE CINEMA SO THEY CAN CHUCK STUFF AT PEOPLE'S HEADS.**

✿ If it's a gross film and girls are with them they enjoy that 'cos girls get scared. They might get a kiss and a cuddle.

✿ They like action, horror films, violent films – stuff that they're too young for. If somebody's head gets chopped off they go, 'oh yeah.'

✿ You get boys in groups watching girly films. They're not interested in the romance, but they like the sex.

✿ They like theme parks and they go to music festivals.

What sort of entertainment do GIRLS like?

★ **THEY LISTEN TO REALLY SOPPY MUSIC.**
★ They like chick flicks – sad films about relationships and romance.
★ They like to go with a lad to watch a romantic film. They sit in the back row, getting with each other.
★ They like watching the boys play sport. Looking at their legs, their muscles, their bums.
★ They like any kind of bar – to have a drink with their mates and find older boys.

Where would BOYS go for a night out?

✿ **THEY HANG AROUND THE TOILETS. IT'S REALLY SAD.**
✿ On week nights they go to the off-licence and get drunk.
✿ To the park – because it's free.
✿ They try to scab drinks from their parents. Half the time they don't drink . . . they just throw the bottles around, but they think it looks cool to have them.
✿ To the cricket club, skateboard park or out on their bikes.
✿ To a night club if they can get in. If they don't get in they show off and say they did get in.
✿ To discos at youth centres.
✿ They sit at their mate's house watching porn.

✿ Their idea of a night out is fish and chips and eating them on a park bench.

✿ They could have a party at their house. It'll be all boys at first . . . then they invite the girls when they get bored.

✿ They're on their PlayStations, or swapping the latest games.

✿ A party or a rave.

✿ To town. They sit on the market stalls – they smoke, eat McDonald's and talk about girls and sometimes drink. They get chased by the police. They think it's cool.

✿ They just mess about smashing windows.

Where would GIRLS go for a night out?

★ **TO A PARTY, A SLEEPOVER, OR CLUBBING.**

★ They hang around the parks and street corners, drinking, smoking and trying to look cool to get off with boys.

★ To discos and cinemas.

★ Some girls have free houses. They take drink there and invite boys in, and they get drunk and then have sex.

★ To a night club – they dress up fancy, thinking that they're it, but they end up just standing there doing nothing.

★ They go down to the garages and get drunk.

★ They'll sit in a phone box and then, when a nice bloke comes along, they ask him if he can buy them some cigarettes. Then they kiss him when he comes back.

★ They might have a girls' night in and talk about boys.
★ To the chip shop.

Where would BOYS go at the weekend?

✿ **THEY WALK THE STREETS LOOKING FOR GIRLS OR TROUBLE.**

✿ To the same places, they don't really change.

✿ It depends where you live – there isn't really anywhere to go.

✿ They probably sit on a wall all day. They drink and get bladdered. Then they walk round town telling people who's the fittest out of a couple of girls.

✿ To play or watch football or rugby.

✿ They have competitions to see who can spend the longest swimming in the river.

✿ They hang about outside McDonald's. They go in and try and steal something.

✿ Some can get into clubs because they look older than they are.

Where would GIRLS go at the weekend?

★ **SHOPPING, OBVIOUSLY.**
  IT'S IN THEIR BRAIN TO SHOP.

★ They always go shopping – they never go anywhere else. They think they need new clothes to impress the boys. Boys always wear clothes more than once. Girls wouldn't be seen dead in clothes they've worn more than once. They go out to buy one thing and come back with full shopping bags.

★ To a sleepover – to watch videos and ring boys up at all hours.

★ They go round the town to be seen.

★ Go for a makeover to try and look nicer for the boys – they want to pull us.

★ They love shopping. They love to look good, so they need to get as many clothes as possible. Even if they haven't got any money they try on clothes.

★ Girls dress up to look as old as they can. 2% of Year Eight look really mature and can get into clubs. They're lucky, they have features that make them look older, like their hair and their breasts, that boys don't. They show their cleavage to the bouncers on the door and they get in.

★ When boys go shopping they know what they're going to get. Girls keep going round for about eight hours. They have to go in a shop about five times before they actually buy something.

What are BOYS like at parties?

✿ **IT'S HANDS UP TOP, HANDS DOWN SKIRT, TONGUES DOWN THROAT.**

✿ Lads act like a bunch of idiots. They're loud. They try and dance with us. They're not embarrassed.

✿ Some boys take their shirts off – to show off to people they fancy. They think it will impress the girls, but it doesn't.

> They show off. They try and flirt with the girls.

✿ They can't dance. They just sit there nodding their heads – like a nodding dog in a car window. Or they do funny things with their feet. They sit and dance with their feet.

✿ A proper lad is a lad who'll have the last dance with you.

✿ They have a competition to see who can kiss the most girls and they put dots on their hands to show their mates how many girls they've kissed.

✿ They don't dance, they jump. The only dance they actually do is the last dance, and even then it's with each other.

✿ They're on one side and the girls are on the other side and they don't talk to each other.

✿ Sometimes the boys get all shy and they'll get their pal to go and ask, 'Would you dance with my mate?'

✿ They dress up cool and gel their hair back and say, 'I want to show you something . . .' and then they take you into a room.

- They feel girls up in the dark.
- They drink booze in front of you and smoke – to make them look older. They think they're all right – 'I'm cool, I'm better than you, so just move out of my face' – but at the end of the day there's only one thing they want and that's sleeping with a girl.

What are GIRLS like at parties?

★ **THEY FLIRT MORE THAN THE BOYS FLIRT.**

★ They say things like, 'You're the sexiest' – and the boys fall for it ('fraid so). They ask you out, but then next day they say they don't want to go out after all. They end up totally ripping your heart out.

★ They pull you up and try to get you to dance. They say you're boring if you don't.

★ They grab you and snog you for no reason. They bet how many people they'll get off with.

★ They try to show off by dancing. When they're dancing they all stand in a circle. They feel as a union together. They kiss and hug each other.

★ They come up and grab your arse at a disco, then they laugh and run off. They say you've been feeling theirs and when you say, 'No, you've been feeling mine,' they call you a 'big bum feeler' and it gets you dead annoyed.

★ Some girls will go off with you into another room.

★ They giggle a lot.

★ They'll wait for the boy to ask them to dance.

★ They try to impress boys all the time. They try to show off by making fun of people.

★ They try to act hard by drinking alcohol.

★ When they're drunk they're all over you. When they're sober they regret it.

★ They take off their shoes when they dance because if they've got really high heels they'll fall over and everyone will laugh at them. They put their bag and their shoes in the middle of the floor and dance round them.

What sort of holiday would appeal to BOYS?

✿ **ANYWHERE WITH GIRLS IN BIKINIS. ALL BOYS ARE PERVERTS.**

✿ They like Ibiza or Spain for the nude beaches.

❀ Ibiza because they can go clubbing and they can stay up all night and get drunk.

❀ Somewhere they can play pinball and pool a lot.

❀ They think they could go clubbing. But they're just dreaming: they'd probably just sit in a restaurant with their mums.

❀ They say they're going to Ibiza to do football training but really they're going to play with their friends and go on the beach and make sand castles and that sort of stupid stuff.

❀ Somewhere they can get a tan and check out the girls.

❀ They stay on the beach – they hardly ever go in the sea, but if they do it's, like, who can get there first and who can swim out the furthest. They show off, jumping over the waves, surfing.

❀ Somewhere with their own room – so they can use the phone and have parties.

What sort of holiday would appeal to GIRLS?

★ **IBIZA BECAUSE OF ALL THE BOYS, CLUBS, PARTIES AND SUN.**

★ Somewhere hot so they get a suntan. It's all they think about. They want to look more attractive to boys. Girls lie there, and we sit and watch the girls.

★ They like to go on holiday with their friends.

★ They're too lazy to do skiing or anything.

★ Somewhere where there's lots of entertainment and lots of shops, like New York or Hong Kong.

★ Where the shops are really cheap so they can buy designer stuff cheaply.

★ They want to get as far away from their parents as possible.

★ They might want to go to a nudist beach or go topless to show off to the boys.

★ Something romantic like a cruise – they'd like the waves splashing against the side of the boat and they'd like to see the dolphins.

★ They want to get a tan in the morning, go shopping in the afternoon and go to a night club at night. They still spend half their days combing their hair even on holiday!

What sports do BOYS do?

✿ ANY SPORT WITH BALLS.

✿ They say they like swimming but it's only because they like to see girls in their swimsuits. They don't like being seen in their trunks.

What sports do GIRLS do?

★ SWIMMING – THEY THINK THEY LOOK SEXY IN THEIR BIKINIS.

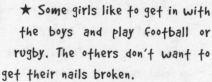

★ Netball – it's girlish because you can't run about. It's not a very fast game – you've got to stand on the spot and throw the ball. They like it because they don't have to move very much. They're lazy.

RUGBY

★ Some girls like to get in with the boys and play football or rugby. The others don't want to get their nails broken.

Are BOYS better at sport?

❀ **BOYS ARE TOO SCARED TO TAKE GIRLS ON IN CASE THEY LOSE.**

❀ No. Most of the girls represent the school. None of the boys do. So girls must be better.

❀ They're better at football or rugby – it's their kind of sport.

❀ Boys are quite sexist – they won't let girls play. That's why the girls nick the balls – to get their own back.

❀ They don't like it if you're fitter than them or better than them at tennis or football.

❀ They think they're good at every single sport, and we can only do girls' sports, but that's rubbish.

 ## Are GIRLS better at sport?

★ **GIRLS CAN'T THROW, THEY CAN'T RUN, THEY'RE USELESS.**

★ Boys are better than girls. Boys practise more. Girls don't want to get sweaty and hot and they don't want to get their knees dirty.

★ They're no good at football because it's physical. They don't like the contact. They're delicate, they don't like getting hurt. It's more of a manly sport. Their nails break, they mess their hair up, they don't want to get dirty. You never see a girl sliding under your feet in a tackle.

How do BOYS behave on the sports field?

✿ **THEY'RE MORE COMPETITIVE. THEY'RE BIG HEADED.**

✿ When you get to the sports field they're so serious it's scary. They feel they have to win everything to be good.

✿ They shout and swear at each other. They need to calm down a bit and **THINK** about what they're doing.

✿ They show off to the girls and to their mates.

✿ They're really bad losers; if you beat them they go off in a huff. But when they win they boast.

✿ They're serious about their sport – a lot of boys think sports are more important than girls.

✿ It's only a game. With girls after a game it's all forgotten. Lads carry it on for ever – they go on and on, 'Ha, we won, we won.' Girls will work together well, lads will go against each other. We can work as a team. They're better at football – it's a team game, but if someone scores a goal it's like they won, not the team won.

✿ When you're running, they'll laugh at you and imitate the way you run.

✿ If you miss a goal then they totally laugh their heads off.

✿ They say, 'Look at me, I'm best,' then they lose.

How do GIRLS behave on the sports field?

★ **GIRLS TRY TO RUN IN LITTLE HUDDLES.**

★ They don't like doing sport. They're not as competitive. They walk around in groups, saying, 'Why should we be doing this?'

They're scared of stupid things like breaking their nails or getting their hair messy.

★ They can't be bothered. They'll say it's too cold.

★ They don't want to get their trainers muddy.

★ Girls don't like running. They don't like doing sport in front of the lads because they want to look their best. They get embarrassed because they've got flabby legs. And it's because of their breasts as well – some girls like their breasts to jump up and down to make the boys like them better, but other girls don't like it.

★ If they've got a PE skirt they push it together between their legs and jog.

★ When they're throwing a ball it's like they're having an attack of something. They don't move their upper arm.

★ They don't like sport because they're too bothered about their hair and their make-up.

What do BOYS read?

✿ **THEY WON'T READ A NOVEL UNLESS IT'S GOT SEX IN IT.**

✿ Porn magazines. They have to look at pictures of nude women because they'll never get to see a real woman – they're never going to get that close to one.

✿ War magazines. They paint little plastic men and have fake battles with them.

✿ They look at girls' magazines to find out what we're up to. They read the problem pages, then take the mickey and laugh at the problems girls have.

✿ They read the walk-through for a computer game – it's the only time they read a whole book.

✿ Some might want to read more interesting books but it would ruin their image. Boys don't read much unless they're a boff or a nerd or a geek.

✿ They get thrills by looking at porno mags and they enjoy shoving them in your face. If there's pictures of naked men they complain. There's different rules for boys and girls. If we bring in pictures of men in underwear they're like, 'oh, my God . . . It's disgusting.' But they're drooling over pictures of women in bras.

PlayStation magazines –
to get the cheats.

What do GIRLS read?

★ **SLOPPY, ROMANTIC STUFF.**
★ They show you what they're reading if it's got swear words.
★ They buy a magazine to get a free lipstick.
★ They read more than boys. But the girls that think they're cool don't read as much.
★ Girlie magazines to find out how to get boys and what boys like. They're looking for tips about how to improve stuff like their make-up, their hair, and their health.

★ They read magazines because they want to find out about condoms and things - because they're getting ready for sex. They read the problems - the sex problems for eighteen-year-olds.
★ When we go to the library, girls come back with a book, the boys don't. We just have a chat when we're down there.
★ They read problem pages because they want to know if they're normal. If boys have got a problem we sort it for ourselves. Girls - they got to talk about it.

Do BOYS get the same amount of pocket money as GIRLS?

✿ THEY GET MORE, AND THEY DON'T DO ANYTHING FOR IT.

✿ Boys get less pocket money than girls because boys get paid more when they do Saturday jobs.

✿ I think they get more – it's to get them out of the house.

> Girls get more because they have jobs. Boys can't be bothered. They'd rather just sit watching telly.

Do GIRLS get the same amount of pocket money as BOYS?

★ THEY GET MORE, BECAUSE THEY SUCK UP TO THEIR PARENTS.

★ They get more, because they do more around the house.

★ They scab off you, or get it from their dads.

What do BOYS spend it on?

✿ **THE LATEST FOOTBALL STRIP.**
✿ Video games.
✿ Porno mags.
✿ Games, sweets, phone cards, cigarettes.
✿ Girls have more things to spend it on. We love shopping. Boys hate it.

What do GIRLS spend it on?

★ **CLOTHES, LIPPY AND NAIL VARNISH.**
★ Phone cards, make-up, accessories and tampons because they might be embarrassed to tell their parents they need them.
★ Drugs like weed and poppers. Not proper drugs.
★ Boys save up and get something big. Girls spend it straight away on little things like CDs and teddies.

abc 296/2

talking
dirty

bleeep!
bleeep!

Do BOYS have any habits that you dislike?

❀ **THEY'RE ALWAYS SCRATCHING THEIR FAMILY JEWELS.**

❀ They eat like they've never been fed before.

❀ You don't even want to see what some of the boys do. They'll get a cheese sandwich and they'll put salt and vinegar crisps and tomato ketchup in it and they'll sit there and eat it in front of you.

❀ It's the manners - eating with their mouths open, slurping and burping. Talking and eating at the same time. It's disgusting. You can see everything.

❀ Half their food's hanging out of their mouth. They spray it everywhere.

❀ They buy bags of chips - then spend most of their time throwing the chips at each other.

❀ They don't use knives and forks. They pick food up with their fingers.

❀ They wipe their mouths on their sleeves.

❀ They spit their drink at each other.

✿ They backwash their drinks – they take it in their mouths and then spit it back in the cup or whatever.

✿ They drink and they burp. And girls are,'That's horrible,' and they just laugh about it.

✿ They have competitions: how far in the alphabet they can get by burping, and who can do the loudest and longest one.

✿ They pick their noses, put their hands down their trousers and wipe their noses on their ties.

✿ They're always playing with their tackle. They always have their hands in their pockets. They know they're doing it. They'd complain if we went around doing it. If we went anywhere near any of our bits they'd go, 'oh my God, what are you doing?' 'Well, excuse me, you're never out of your pants . . .'

✿ They always scratch their bums.

- They spit in front of you and they do greenies in front of you – ugh!
- They stick their hands down their trousers and feel around and they carry on as if it's just normal. They do it in class.
- They put stuff down their trousers to make their things look bigger – rulers and pencils.

- They measure their bits down the phone to you.
- They go on about shaving – 'oh, yeah, we shave all the time' – no, you don't.
- They don't care where they fart. They don't do it in private, they do it in public and laugh about it.
- They wear too much of their spray things.

Do GIRLS have any habits that you dislike?

★ **SOME OF THEM PICK THEIR NOSES AND EAT IT.**

★ When they eat they're just too nice – they don't just eat . . . they cut everything up into really small pieces – even their chips!

★ Crisps – boys take a handful, girls take one or two crisps at a time. They don't want to put their hands in because of their nails – they don't want to break them or something.

★ They spend ages trying to eat something. They take tiny bites so their mouth doesn't look big. They want to look more feminine so they take little nibbles.

Girls have a go at us for picking our noses, but they do it too!

★ When girls drink they go gently, so they don't get lipstick over everything.
★ They sip instead of gulp. And they don't burp!
★ They fart. But if you're going out with them and you say, 'Ah, you just farted,' they'll say 'We're finished.'
★ They stick their little finger up when they drink like they're all posh and goody-goody.

★ They're always doing their nails. They have things like diamonds on them and it's really sad.
★ They open their mouths wide to shout, but they eat with small mouths.

★ I don't like them standing on the street corner and drinking.
★ They drink because they want to act hard in front of the lads. But it's two mouthfuls and then they're drunk. It's disgusting when they're sick afterwards.
★ They try to act hard and pretend they're drunk when they're not. Then they take advantage of the boys – and start kissing them.

I hate cracking fingers!

Girls bite their nails!

★ I can't stand girls that drink in front of boys. They turn into tarts when they drink.

★ They're forever combing their hair with these big brushes. And they're always shaking and twisting it about. It gets in your face or in your dinner.

★ They write on their arm things like i love ****. It's really annoying – if you're going to write it, you might as well say out loud. It's really childish.

★ When they're chewing gum they pull it out, wrap it round their fingers then put it back in and sometimes they get big slavers on their fingers.

abc 296/2

getting together

bleeep!
bleeep!

What do BOYS do that you do like?

✿ **THEY CAN BE QUITE FUNNY SOMETIMES.**

✿ They play football!

✿ Sometimes they will say sorry if they do something you don't like.

✿ They'll stick up for you.

✿ If you're crying in the classroom they will come up and ask if you're all right.

✿ The boffin ones can help you with your homework.

✿ They smile at you.

✿ Some are sweet, but that's very few. You're lucky if you find a sweet one.

✿ They can be charming and sweet – once in a million years.

✿ When they just come up and hug you and they don't want anything else.

✿ Sometimes they play with your hair.

They flirt with you!

What do GIRLS do that you do like?

★ **IF THEY'RE A GOOD KISSER.**
★ When they smile at you.
★ It's good when they flash a bit.
★ When they're straightforward, not sarky or anything.
★ They like having a laugh with boys.
★ They cuddle and kiss you.

★ When they pull up their tights or adjust their bras.
  It's nice and very distracting!
★ When they move their hips.
★ I like the way some girls keep themselves to themselves –
  and don't talk about other people.

Do BOYS enjoy working with GIRLS?

✿ **BOYS CAN'T CONCENTRATE WHEN THEY'RE WITH GIRLS.**

✿ They like working with girls if they fancy them or if they're really good friends.

✿ They'd rather work with other boys and gang up on girls.

✿ They'd worry about how they smelt, or about their hair.

✿ They find it funny and slag girls off and take the mickey.

✿ They like doing PE with girls, because girls have little skirts on.

Do GIRLS enjoy working with BOYS?

★ **THEY LIKE TO FLIRT AND SHOW OFF TO THE BOYS THEY FANCY.**

★ They want to work with boys during PE because they want to 'perv' on them.

★ Yes, because they know the lad knows more.

★ If a girl is friends with you or likes you, she may want to work with you, but if not she'd rather work with her lassie friends.

★ If they fancy a boy they'll go and sit by him intentionally but at the same time say, 'I don't want to sit by him . . .' Then they punch him, and beat him up just to touch him.

Is it possible to make friends with a BOY your age?

✿ **YES - IF THEY CAN MAKE YOU LAUGH WHEN YOU'RE SAD.**

✿ Yes, but other people tease you - they think you must be going out with him.

✿ They can listen to you just as well as girls can. Sometimes they listen better.

✿ If you've got a special friendship with a boy you can tell secrets to him and you can trust him not to tell.

✿ It's easy to be friends with a gay boy because he's not going to try anything on.

✿ You can trust most gay boys better than straight boys. He's a bit like a girl. He's more feminine. He's like a friend. He can share your feelings.

✿ Sometimes it's easier to get on with a boy because girls are bitchy. With boys you can have a laugh.

✿ You can become close friends with someone you've been out with.

✿ Some boys you can stay friends with for ages.

What would you expect from that friendship?

✿ **YOU CAN TELL THEM STUFF AND THEY CAN TELL YOU STUFF.**

✿ If you fancied one of his mates he would set him up with you.

✿ He doesn't mind saying to other people that he's friends with you and he isn't afraid to speak to you when his friends are there.

✿ He'd stick up for you if you're in trouble.

✿ Their respect – so they won't go around making fun of you.

✿ They're not afraid to cry in front of you. And you'd want to be able to cry on them as well.

And what would destroy it?

❀ **IF THEY TELL YOUR SECRETS TO THEIR FRIENDS.**

❀ If he started fancying you, or if you'd been friends with him and then you started fancying him, you wouldn't feel comfortable any more.

❀ If he slagged you off.

❀ If he makes up rumours that you and he have done something when you haven't - you're just friends.

❀ If he likes making fun of you.

❀ If they completely change when they're with their friends; they're so horrible when they get with their mates.

❀ If he's two-faced to you.

❀ If you started going out with him then you split up, you'd break friends as well.

❀ If he was going out with somebody and he chose them over you.

❀ If he was going out with one of your mates and he went with someone else and you knew. You wouldn't know what to do.

❀ If they blame you for things they've done.

Is it possible to make friends with a GIRL your age?

★ **YOU CAN WITH SOME, BUT OTHERS WANT TO MAKE MORE OF IT.**

★ Some want to be friends and hang around with you, and other girls want you to go out with them and give them all your money so they can go shopping.

★ Sometimes you've been brought up with a girl and so she's just your mate.

★ No, because of their friends – they say, 'oh, you don't want to go round with him.'

★ Yes, with a tomboy.

★ If you share an interest with them – like music or sport.

What would you expect from that friendship?

★ **THAT SHE'D DANCE WITH YOU AT A DISCO.**

★ You'd expect the same from that friendship as from a boy.

★ To be able to trust her.

★ You'd want her to be loyal, thoughtful, comforting.

★ Truth, honesty and humour.

★ Sometimes if you want to go out with another girl, you want advice like, 'Do you think this suits me?' 'What does she like – does she like a tough-man attitude or a nice, soft, wimpy attitude?'

★ You can ask her for advice — what do girls do, what do they like, what don't they like, how do they think?

And what would destroy it?

★ **IF SUDDENLY YOU FANCIED HER AND TRIED TO HIT ON HER.**

★ If she talked about you behind your back.

★ If she gets a new mate, and you say you don't like her then that'll be the end of your friendship.

★ If she tried to make friends with a different boy so you felt left out.

★ If she made a pass at you when she's told you to leave her alone. You'd be confused.

★ If you told them a secret and they told other people.

★ If they went away with somebody else and only used you when there was nobody else there.

★ If she goes out with your best friend or your enemy.

★ If they went off with someone else when they were supposed to be doing something with you.

★ If you started going out with each other and then split up, you could never be friends again.

★ If you had a relationship with her best friend, because if you broke up it would ruin it.

> ## In what ways are BOYS' friendships different to GIRLS'

❀ **BOYS DON'T HOLD GRUDGES LIKE GIRLS DO.**

❀ Boys never fall out, or if they do, they have a quick fight about it, then they're friends again. Girls seem to argue more.

❀ Boys have loads of friends and get on better in groups than girls do. But they only have one or two close friends.

❀ When girls fall out they bring up things that happened years ago – boys can't remember what happened last week.

❀ Lads can't talk to each other. They think that other lads haven't got any feelings, they make jokes about everything.

❀ Boys get uptight when they hear someone's bitched about them. Girls just accept it because they do it all the time.

❀ Boys can't tell each other problems because their mate would think the other one was weaker.

> ## In what way are GIRLS' friendships different to BOYS'?

★ **GIRLS MAKE FRIENDS EASILY AND THEY FALL OUT EASILY AS WELL.**

★ Girls share their secrets more and keep each other's secrets. Boys can't share secrets: they think it's funny and they tell someone else.

★ Girls care about their friends more. They're more lovey-dovey, they kiss each other.

> Boys have more to relate to each other, girls only have make-up and shopping.

★ Girls fall out and make up a couple of days later. Boys are more serious, they have a big fight at the end.
★ Girls go arguing on and on. If boys have a fight they make it up the next day.

★ Girls are always round each other's houses. They read each other's diaries and love letters and things.
★ Girls are more honest with each other. Boys are embarrassed about stuff.
★ Girls don't compete with their friends like boys do.
★ Girls always fall out. Boys muck around with each other, they don't have any reason to fall out. Girls argue over daft things like make-up.

abc   296/2
getting on

bleeep!
bleeep!

When did you first think about going out with a BOY?

✿ WHEN WE STARTED PLAYING KISS-CHASE.

✿ When you first start primary school you have a pretend marriage. You don't properly go out with them until Years five and six.

✿ I can't remember that far back.

When did you first think of going out with a GIRL?

★ WHEN YOUR FRIENDS ARE GOING OUT WITH GIRLS AND YOU'RE NOT.

★ When you're little, you don't know what you're doing. You don't really want to go out with her, but you want to look at her.

★ Probably about nine/ten years old. You have playground relationships, but you don't go anywhere outside school.

★ When my grandad asked if I was going out with someone.

Do BOYS look for GIRLS the same age as them?

✿ **BOYS LOOK FOR OLDER GIRLS - THEY'VE GOT BIGGER BITS.**

✿ It depends what height they are - if they're really tall they'll go for older girls. If not, they look for someone the same height. It would make him feel small if a girl was taller than him. And it's hard to kiss.

✿ Girls the same age or older - because they've got bigger tits. They're more experienced.

Do GIRLS look for BOYS the same age as them?

★ **THEY THINK IT'S COOL TO GO OUT WITH SOMEONE OLDER.**

★ older boys because they have more money to take them out and take them shopping.

★ They look for older boys - because they've got more money and bigger bits.

★ older boys because they're at the same level of maturity.

Who should do the asking out?

✿ **BOYS ARE SCARED OF REJECTION.**

✿ I don't think it matters that much. It could be either of them.

✿ A lot of boys can't pluck up the courage to ask you out, so they ask their friends to do it for them.

✿ Sometimes their friends will ask you to go out with a boy even though he hasn't asked them to. It's a game.

✿ Boys, but it shouldn't always be up to the boys. We're strong women, we should take charge sometimes.

✿ We wouldn't dare. If the girl asks it makes the girl look desperate. A girl takes it more seriously: if the boy asks and is turned down he's not bothered, but if a girl asks and she's turned down it kind of hurts them.

Who should do the asking out?

★ **SOMETIMES GIRLS GET THEIR MATES TO ASK YOU OUT.**
★ Girls haven't got the guts to ask a boy out, but it would be good if they did.
★ Boys always have to do it.
★ Girls get embarrassed or sad if they're turned down.
★ Boys are more confident with it; girls are all shy. It would break the tradition.

What do you think turns a BOY on about you?

✿ **PRETTY LOOKS. NICE BUM. GREAT LEGS.**
✿ How fit you are - like big tits. They ask what your bra size is.
✿ Short skirts.
✿ Personality - someone they can talk to.

What do you think turns a GIRL on about you?

★ **EYES - IT'S JUST A GIRL THING. EYES ARE MYSTICAL.**

★ The way you look and the way you act. You have to be cool.

★ You've got to have a good personality and be good to talk to.

★ You're not allowed to be forward going - like snogging: I want to start doing this, she doesn't. You have to be patient.

★ If you're good friends, sporty and good-looking. They like muscles, legs, taller boys, a nice bum, a six-pack.

★ Boys who are funny, cute, caring and with a good attitude.

★ Your face, and if they like you after that, it's what you do with them.

★ Putting your arm round her. Playing around with her nipples. Girls have got spots on the back of their neck, and the back of their arms. You have to give them a good rub.

What turns you on about a BOY?

✿ **I LIKE THEIR HAIRY LEGS.**

✿ First it's looks. If they pass the looks test then it's personality. Personality is an added bonus.

✿ A nice tanned, hairless chest. Nice neck, back, hair. Nice face, nice bum!

✿ Nice eyes so you get drawn into them.

🌸 A six-pack!

🌸 He's got to have a sensitive side and he's got to be quite popular. Not a geek.

🌸 I don't care about looks – it's personality.

🌸 If he's sensitive and understands feelings.

🌸 A good sense of humour.

🌸 If they treat you decently.

What turns you on about a GIRL?

★ **I THINK GOD PUT LASSES ON THE PLANET TO TEASE US LADS.**

★ If she talks slowly and gently.

★ Big breasts and nice long, tanned legs.

★ When they push out their chests and brush their hair behind their shoulders.

★ Nice, long, straight, blonde hair, blue eyes.
★ Short skirts, tight tops with a low cleavage and high heels.

★ When they drink Coke, they have it in a cup with a straw so they can act up when they're sucking the straw.
★ When a girl flicks her hair and bites her bottom lip, then she looks at you with her head on one side and winks.
★ If she's got her finger in her mouth and she looks at you.

What puts you off a BOY?

✿ **HAIRY, SMELLY ARMPITS - oof!**
✿ If he's always moaning.
✿ A bad attitude. If they've got an attitude problem then they can forget it.
✿ If they cheat on other girls really badly.
✿ I don't like hairy chests or backs. You get your fingers lost in his hairs.
✿ Some boys have flab and it's horrible. It hangs down and wobbles when they walk. They've got bigger boobs than you have!

Hairy bums!

* If they're too thin they just look long and lanky.
* Their hands are always dirty.
* Greasy hair, or hair with too much gel on it.
* I don't like sweaty hands. You can't hold them - they're always slipping away.
* Thick eyebrows that join in the middle.
* Spots or scars or craters!
* I don't like the look of boys' feet. They're big and ugly and I don't like the hairs.
* Their feet are sweaty and bony. They get athlete's foot, they don't look after their feet like girls do, they've got dirt under their toenails.
* Toenails - because they're all nasty and horrible, like they curl under and they never can be bothered to cut them.
* If they've got holes in their clothes or trainers, or if they're dirty. Some boys don't care - they still wear them.

What would put you off snogging a BOY?

* **A WASHING-MACHINE TONGUE GOING ROUND FAST.**
* What they eat: really disgusting combinations, and things like pickled onion, crisps or garlic bread.
* Teeth - sometimes they don't brush them. Yellow, crooked teeth make me sick.

❀ If you hear rumours he shoves his tongue down your throat. or bites your tongue or has bad breath.

❀ Cold sores, cracked lips, or big lips.

❀ It's horrible when they need a shave. It's prickly and you go home with a burning chin.

 What puts you off a GIRL?

★ **YOU CAN'T GO WALKING AROUND WITH A MINGER!**

★ If a girl's a lot fatter, you're not usually attracted to her.

★ If you thought she was a girly girl, but she turns out to be a manly girl and she's got bruises on her legs.

★ If they're always moaning and nit-picking.

★ If she's got to be always in charge.

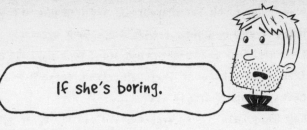

If she's boring.

★ If they're really boastful.
★ If they're standing there in your face and you're not interested, you want to say, 'I'm not interested in your body, it's what I feel for you and what you feel for me that's important.'
★ Hairy armpits.
★ If they have moles or nasty birthmarks.
★ Their nails are always long and scratchy all the time. That's scary!
★ Spots on their face – they could use clearasil or disguise them with make-up.
★ When their faces are ten times as thick as they really are with make-up and it looks like a plastic mask.
★ They shave everywhere else, but then they've still got hairy arms.
★ Their arms – they swing them from the elbows as if they're doing weights.

★ When they pluck their eyebrows and look like the devil.

★ They pile stuff on their eyelids, pluck their eyebrows and do their lips! Then they start crying and it runs and looks awful.

★ Their feet - because they paint their toenails.

★ Cheesy, smelly, crusty feet.

★ Hair that hasn't been washed, and tangled up or straggly hair is horrible.

★ Long hair, because they're always flicking it in your face.

★ I don't like girls with short hair like boys, it puts you off.

★ Fat, hairy legs.

★ Some girls' legs are fat and wrinkly - they need to be nice and brown.

★ I hate it when horrible lasses wear their skirts up to there and when they sit down, and they've got no tights on, their legs look like salami.

★ I hate it when flat-chested lasses wear tight tops - they haven't got anything to show off.

What would put you off snogging a GIRL?

★ **WHEN THEY SNOG LIKE A FISH WITH THEIR MOUTHS WIDE OPEN.**

★ Cold sores, eczema or spots.

★ Bad breath - they're always chewing gum to make their breath smell good. It kind of indicates their breath is bad.

★ When they bite your lips.

★ When you pull away and they spit.

★ Yellow teeth, cracked lips, or braces that slip down. They might come out when you're snogging her.

★ If she's got three weeks worth of food in her braces, or crisps stuck in her teeth.

★ A runny nose or bogies hanging down.

★ If somebody else told you they weren't very good at it.

★ A big tongue that chops you when you're snogging.

What sort of presents do BOYS give you?

✿ **CHOCOLATES, FLOWERS OR REALLY RUDE UNDERWEAR.**

✿ Jewellery - earrings, or a necklace with a heart on it.

✿ They try to buy you clothes but they're three sizes too big!

✿ Chocolates or jellies of rude parts.

❖ Some boys give you what their mum has got for them to give you – a teddy.

❖ A flower, one single little rose.

❖ Sometimes boys say, 'I was going to get you something but I didn't have the money,' or they say they left the present at home, or they forget.

❖ A little ornament with '**I LOVE YOU**' on it.

What sort of presents do GIRLS give you?

★ A necklace with '**I LOVE YOU**' on.

★ A teddy bear holding a heart thing that says something like '**MY HEART IS YOUR HEART**', or '**COME OVER TONIGHT AND I'LL GIVE YOU A SNOG**'.

★ The chocolate they put on and you lick off.

★ A big giant pair of tits, but it's a lolly so you lick it.

★ They wouldn't get us anything, but they expect roses and chocolates and stuff like that from us.

★ Clothes that they think you look better in.

★ Really soppy presents like little cuddly toys that they think you're going to like and you don't really want, but you take it because you don't want to hurt their feelings.

★ Boxers – she might get to see them on you, you never know . . .

What might a BOY give you for a special anniversary? One month?

✿ **THEY'D FORGET. THEY PROBABLY WOULDN'T EVEN CARE.**

✿ Nothing – they wouldn't even know they'd been going out for a month.

✿ If he was nagged into taking her out he'd probably take her to a football match and buy her some fish and chips.

Six months?

✿ HE WOULDN'T EVEN REMEMBER IT. YOU'D HAVE
TO TELL HIM. HE'D PROBABLY SAY, 'OH, RIGHT.'

**What might a GIRL give you
for a special anniversary?
One month?**

★ **A BIG FAT KISS.**
★ Maybe a card, maybe a ring, maybe chocolate
or a note saying, 'I love you'.

★ She wouldn't buy you a present. It's a silly anniversary.
★ The girls would know because they keep everything in a
diary. But if you forget it you might get dumped.
★ Nothing – a month is nothing.

Six months?

★ A T-SHIRT. AND IF YOU DON'T WEAR IT YOU'RE FINISHED.

★ Jewellery.

★ Girls get you something and you think, 'What am I going to do with this?'

bleeep!
bleeep!

in your dreams

What sort of secrets do BOYS have?

✿ **WHO THEY FANCY.**
✿ What they think about girls.
✿ That they've kept their teddy bears.
✿ That they're still virgins.
✿ They're going out with someone and they fancy someone else.

I'd like to know what boys think!

What sort of secrets do GIRLS have?

★ **IT'S ALL BOYS.**
★ They fancy a boy but don't want to tell him.
★ A friend's secret.

What do BOYS daydream about?

✿ **GIRLS AND FOOTBALL.**
✿ Nude girls.
✿ Motorbikes and girls' bits.
✿ Girls, boobs and sex.

What do GIRLS daydream about?

★ **BOYS AND SHOPPING.**
★ Pop stars.
★ Sex when they're older.
★ Getting married.
★ God knows!

What do BOYS lie about?

✿ **BOYS LIE AND CHEAT ALL THE TIME.**

✿ How many girlfriends they've had. They're always saying, 'I pulled last night.'

✿ How much they love you.

✿ They two-time you.

✿ If they try to chat you up, they lie about what they like. If you say you like fluffy bunnies they'll say they do too.

✿ They pretend they've got girlfriends and they know what they're doing and they really don't.

✿ How big their dick is.

✿ If you were a virgin, they'd say they've had loads of girls.

✿ They always say they've done it with someone on holiday. Then they can't be pinned down to a name.

✿ They lie about how many girls they've had sex with. It's just to fit in with their mates.

✿ They try and impress by saying they're in a football team and they're not.

- If they have a watch they say it's really expensive and you know it's not.
- They say their dad's a millionaire.
- If they go shopping with their mum they'll say they've been to a football match instead.
- They lie about drinking alcohol.
- They lie about their age so you'll go out with them . . . and so they can get into clubs.

What do GIRLS lie about?

★ **WHO THEY GOT OFF WITH AT A PARTY.**

★ They lie when they like a boy because they don't want to let the secret out. That's stupid, though, because if they want to go out with a boy and no one ever knows then they won't be able to go out with him.

★ Sometimes they say one of their friends fancies you, then when you go and ask the girl she'll say she doesn't.

★ They lie about the size of their breasts – they stuff paper in their bras to make them look bigger.

★ They lie about having sex and stuff.

★ They say they haven't got a boyfriend and then you find out they have and you get in fights and stuff.

Girls lie about everything!

★ They'll say they've got a boyfriend as an excuse if they don't like you, or if they're playing hard to get.

★ The end of a relationship - they say they ended it even if they didn't, or if you cheated on them and they found out they say they cheated too. It's to save their pride.

★ Their age - they try to act older than they really are.

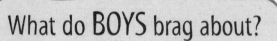

What do BOYS brag about?

✿ **THEY'RE ALWAYS BRAGGING ABOUT THEIR TACKLE.**

✿ A pretty girlfriend. If it was someone who was popular and everyone wanted to go out with her then they'd tell everyone.

Boys say they've done more than they have!

> Boys brag about how many pubes they've got. They count them!

✿ They brag about how far they would go. But when they came down to it I don't think they would go that far.

✿ They're always bragging about **IT**, but when it comes to it they'll say, 'oh, I've got to go now, my dinner's ready.'

✿ Sex - things they get up to with girls. Half of it probably isn't true. They over-exaggerate.

✿ How many push-ups they do.

✿ Winning at things - like a tennis tournament.

What do GIRLS brag about?

★ **BEING BETTER THAN THE BOYS AT ANYTHING.**

★ They brag about most things.

★ How much they had to drink last night. They try to show off by saying they got drunk, but it's no big deal really.

★ New clothes.

★ Bodies – they brag about big breasts.

★ They say, 'I've got this really cool friend who could beat you up,' but he doesn't exist. It's just to make them look hard.

★ In class they start singing to show off their voices.

★ What they do with their boyfriend. It makes them look big. If their friends are doing it and they're not, they have to lie about it.

★ They give a boy a peck, then say, 'I put my tongue down his throat.'

★ Meeting boys. They'll say, 'on holiday I kissed ten boys.'

★ When they say they've done something with a boy they'll talk about his size.

★ They try to impress the boys by saying they smoke.

Girls brag about most things...

What sort of job would a BOY like to have?

❁ **PROFESSIONAL FOOTBALLERS.**
❁ Some boys know exactly what they want to do and work towards it.
❁ They say women should go out and earn the money and they should spend it. And every Friday when they get home from work there should be a curry on the table.
❁ They want to work under cars so they can look up girls' skirts.
❁ Be in a band.

What sort of job would a GIRL like to have?

★ **A MODEL, AN AIR HOSTESS OR NURSE.**
★ A secretary or a waitress. Hairdresser or beautician.
★ In a shop or an office.
★ Looking after children.
★ In a job you have to go from the bottom to the top. Men stick at it. I don't think a girl would.
★ A vet.
★ A well-paid job.

If money and age were no object ... What sort of house would a **BOY** live in?

✿ HE'D HAVE A FLAT AND A REALLY POSH CAR.
✿ A big one, but it'd be messy. He'd never clean it. There'd be dishes lying about, and when his mum came round he'd say, 'oh, Mum, can you iron my shirts for me 'cos I'm going out.'
✿ A mansion with a big double bed to bring girls back and there'd be alcohol everywhere.

What sort of vehicle would he have?

✿ A Ferrari, Porsche or a big convertible.
✿ A flashy car to pick up girls and to show off to other boys.

If money and age were no object ... What sort of house would a GIRL live in?

★ **A HUGE, POSH MANSION.**
★ They'd have everything perfect. Like a doll's house. They'd have maids everywhere to do everything. The maids will be men with no tops on.

What sort of vehicle would she have?

★ **A SPORTY CONVERTIBLE – YELLOW, PINK OR SILVER.**
★ coupé, BMW, Ferrari or Lamborghini – it would have to be red. They just love red things. They think it makes them look sexy.
★ They want the fast cars and the four-wheel drives, they wouldn't want anything rattly.
★ Big, massive, posh car that everyone will look at, like a stretch limo.

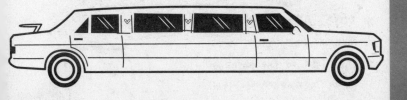

What do BOYS talk about on the phone?

✿ **GIRLS – HOW MANY THEY'VE PULLED.**

✿ They don't have proper conversations. If two boys sit on the phone it's like, 'What?' 'Yeah.'

✿ They never make proper arrangements with each other. They always forget to say something like what time they're going to meet and have to phone again.

✿ Their bikes, football and what they're going to do at the weekend.

✿ They phone sex lines.

What do GIRLS talk about on the phone?

★ **BOYS, AND GOING OUT.**

★ Meeting each other.

★ They'll be on the phone all the time. They never stop talking.

What do BOYS use their mobiles for?

✿ **TO STORE GIRLS' NUMBERS AND PHONE GIRLS.**

✿ They use them to be cool, but they're switched off most of the time.

✿ They pretend to use them but they don't because they're only allowed to use them for emergency calls.

✿ Every week they change their phone to look cool. It's cool to have a good phone, not to have a brick.

✿ Some boys think they're cool, but when they see the big boys they quickly put their phones away and run into shops so no one can steal them.

What do GIRLS use their mobiles for?

★ **TO PHONE BOYS.**

★ For texting – it's not as embarrassing because you don't actually have to talk. They can't dump a boy face to face so they do it by a text message.

★ For emergencies.

★ Popularity – the more ring tones their phone has, and the smaller it is, then they'll be more popular.

★ They pretend they're talking to people on the phone.

What sort of texts do BOYS send?

✿ **STUPID ONES. SOPPY ONES, FLIRTY ONES AND VERY RUDE ONES.**

✿ Football. They send each other the latest scores.

✿ 'I LOVE YOU' messages; poems about 'YOU AND ME' – the thing is, they're not actually written by them. They've been written by somebody else and passed on.

✿ 'I KNOW WHERE YOU LIVE' to a girl to psych her out.

✿ If you send a text message, they only send one word answers because they can't be bothered. So if you wrote 'I LOVE YOU' they'd write back 'OK'.

✿ They send dirty pictures showing little dicks and saying dirty stuff.

What sort of texts do GIRLS send?

★ **DIRTY OR FLIRTY MESSAGES.**

★ About boys – who they fancy, who they like.

★ To ask other girls if they're coming out and where to meet.

★ 'WILL YOU GO OUT WITH ME?'

★ They tell their boyfriends in front of their mates that they don't like them, then use a text message to say, 'I DIDN'T MEAN IT.'

★ Things like, 'I LOVE YOU,' or 'FANCY A QUICKIE?'
★ Things they want to say that they don't want anyone to overhear.

What do BOYS talk about ...at a sleepover?

✿ **THEY'D SIT AND GRUNT - THAT'S ALL LADS DO.**
✿ They discuss how to kiss a girl.
✿ Some of them discuss the bruises they're going to get after wrestling, or stupid things like that.
✿ They talk about football and girls.

When they're getting ready for a party?

✿ **WHAT THEY'RE GOING TO WEAR. IF THEY'RE GOING ON THE PULL.**
✿ What type of gel and aftershave they're going to wear.
✿ They'll say they're going to count the number of girls they get off with.
✿ 'I'm going to get lucky tonight' - they pick out who to go for.
✿ Who they're going to ask to dance. Who they fancy.
✿ 'She came over my house - she let me do this, I let her do this.'

In the BOYS' changing room?

✿ **HOW BIG THEIR MUSCLES ARE.**

✿ Athletics – who got the highest, who ran fastest.

✿ They talk about the way they look – 'You need a bra, you've got bigger boobs than the girls; you need to go to the gym.'

✿ They talk about which girl runs fastest, which girls have got the nicest legs.

✿ They have to have communal showers and they get really embarrassed and don't know where to look.

✿ Their sizes – 'I've got bigger feet, so **MINE'S** bigger than **YOURS.**'

What do GIRLS talk about …at a sleepover?

★ **GIRLIE STUFF - CLOTHES, SEX, HAIR, BREASTS, PERIODS.**

★ Boys: who they've been with, and who they fancy.

★ Who's got the biggest bosoms.

★ Their clothes - 'Do I look right in this?' - that sort of thing.

★ What they should do with a boy - advising each other.

★ They'll discuss hair, or do each other's hair.

When they're getting ready for a party?

★ **TACTICS: HOW THEY'RE GOING TO CHAT UP A BOY.**

★ Their shoes, make-up, clothes.

★ Who they're meeting - what lad they're meeting at the party. What they hope will happen.

★ What boys they're going to ask out, what boys they're going to dance with, who else is going. They'll start bitching about other girls.

★ Boys, bums and hair.

★ 'Does my bum look big in this?' 'Does this look sexy?'

In the GIRLS' changing room?

★ **THE NICE LEGS OF THE LADS IN THE OTHER CHANGING ROOM.**

★ Boys, clothes, hair.

★ 'Does my arse look big in this?'

★ 'There's this lad out there and he's so cute. I want to look sexy.' And they try to make their top dead tight.

★ Their bra size.

★ They're not discussing anything, they're just combing their hair.

★ How they don't want to do the lesson – it's too cold.

★ Swapping make-up – 'It's really nice, try it.'

What sort of websites do BOYS visit?

✿ **CHAT-UP LINES.**

✿ They visit rude porno sites where there's naked women talking to them, telling them to do stuff to themselves!

✿ PlayStation, motorbike and skateboarding sites.

✿ Sites to download music.

What sort of websites do GIRLS visit?

★ **SOAP PAGES AND BOY BANDS.**

★ Teddybear.com.

★ Make-up.com.

★ Shopping.com.

★ They talk to boys on the chatrooms.

★ When they're in a big group they'll visit websites with men, porn sites. They wouldn't do it on their own.

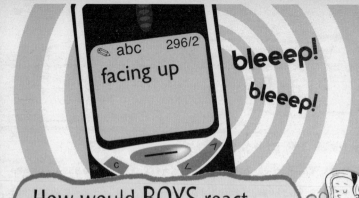

abc 296/2

facing up

bleeep!
bleeep!

How would BOYS react ... if they received an unexpected Valentine's card?

✿ **THEY'D SAY IT WAS FROM THAT REALLY GORGEOUS GIRL IN YEAR TEN.**

✿ They'd love it. It'd make them feel good about themselves.

✿ They'd be showing everyone and boasting about it.

✿ They'd be embarrassed. They pretend they don't want it, but actually they're really chuffed.

✿ He'd do everything in his power to find out who it was from.

✿ If it was from a girl who was really popular, really pretty, he would tell everyone. If it was from someone really ugly – a right nerd – he'd probably rip it up or something.

✿ He wouldn't tell anyone.

✿ They'd make up that it was from a girl they fancied.

If they came face to face with a GIRL they really liked?

✿ **THEY'D GET TONGUE-TIED AND LOOK DOWN AT THE GROUND.**

✿ They'd go bright red. They'd be shy.

✿ They'd freeze; they won't move. They'd stutter or talk in a high voice.

✿ They're cowards. They'd go red and quiet. They'd fiddle with their hair. They'd hide their mouth in their coat and stand there.

✿ Some of them would flirt.

How would GIRLS react … if they received an unexpected Valentine's card?

★ **SHE'D START SCREAMING.**

★ Some would be embarrassed by it. They might go all red.

★ Some would try to find out who it was from. They'd say it was from the most popular boy in the class or say it was an older boy – someone in Year Ten.

★ She'd throw it away.
★ They'd be gob-smacked. They'd go bragging about it to their best friends.

If they came face to face with a BOY they really liked?

★ **THEY'D PANIC, GIGGLE AND STUTTER.**
★ She'd go all red, embarrassed and shy.
★ They'd say stuff they didn't really want to say.
★ They'd run off laughing.
★ They'd let the boy do the talking. They'd try to act cool.

What would scare a BOY?

❀ **BRAS - BECAUSE THEY DON'T KNOW HOW TO UNDO THEM.**

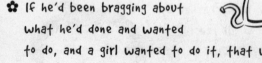

❀ If he'd been bragging about what he'd done and wanted to do, and a girl wanted to do it, that would scare him. A lot of the girls our age have done more than the boys our age.
❀ Boys find girls scary - especially a girl telling him that she loves him.
❀ A girl he really fancied turning him down in front of all his mates.

- ✿ A girl that's really disgusting who he hates comes up and gives him a sloppy kiss.
- ✿ Their enemy's bigger brother.
- ✿ Spiders or snakes.

- ✿ An old lady with nothing on!
- ✿ A harder boy who comes up and starts on him in front of all his friends.
- ✿ High-heeled shoes - they're scared you'll stand on their toes.
- ✿ Girls - because girls are really bitchy and can scratch and bite and things in a fight.
- ✿ Rides in a theme park, but they wouldn't admit it.

What would scare a GIRL?

- ★ BIG, MASSIVE SPIDERS.
- ★ Darkness.
- ★ Wasps and bees and little bugs.
- ★ Snakes, bats and reptiles.

★ If you turned on her and were really up in her face. If you said you were going to get her.
★ Dirty old men. A rapist. A stalker.
★ Being alone in a dark alley.
★ Something that pops out at her round a corner.
★ Scary films.

What makes a BOY laugh?

✿ **THEY LAUGH AT JOKES ABOUT BLONDES.**
✿ If a girl farted.

✿ If someone falls over or does something clumsy. They trip people up and that makes them laugh.
✿ Discussing teachers' underwear.
✿ Dirty jokes.
✿ Girls getting their bits out.
✿ Other people being stupid.
✿ Their friend cussing a girl.
✿ Something embarrassing happening to one of his mates.
✿ At their own jokes – and they're not even funny.
✿ If somebody peed their bed.
✿ Pulling a chair from underneath someone.

What makes a GIRL laugh?

★ **IF YOU PULLED A MOONIE IN FRONT OF HER.**

★ A lad getting in trouble. Boys being beaten up.

★ Boys making fools of themselves.

★ Your face - if you made a silly face.

★ Being silly and mucking around.

★ Dirty jokes.

★ A boy with a stupid piece of clothing on.

★ If someone falls over. If you fall over they call you
   a geek.

★ If your chat-up line fails.

★ The full monty.

★ 'I did it the other night and he's only got a small one.'

★ Girls get the giggles over
   everything.

What makes a BOY cry?

✿ **IF HE GOT KICKED IN THE PRIVATES.**

✿ Boys try not to cry. They try and hide it more; they try not to show their emotions.

✿ Being dumped by someone he really, really liked.

✿ If a boy really likes a girl and she treats him like dirt.

✿ When they get dumped – which is quite often.

✿ If his pet died.

✿ Getting in trouble – they cry when they get suspended.

✿ If someone he loved, like his mum, died or was rushed to hospital.

✿ I don't think they'd cry over a girl. Girls cry over boys, but I don't think boys cry over girls. Some lads might do in their bedroom, but not in public.

✿ Girls cry over movies and stuff, boys don't. Lads might get upset but they'll say, 'oh, this is boring,' so they don't have to watch it. or if they've got tears they'll yawn or say they got something in their eye.

✿ If their bike broke.

✿ If England lost the World Cup.

What makes a GIRL cry?

★ **IF THEIR FAVOURITE BOY BAND BREAKS UP.**
★ If one of their friends gets dumped they'll have a big
   group cry.

★ Split ends and broken nails.
★ If her grandad or someone in her family died.
★ If they've broken up with their boyfriends.
★ You dump her and go with someone else.
★ If she has a fight with her best friend.
★ A really soppy film.
★ If they don't get everything they want.
★ If you say she's fat or she's put on weight.
★ If she's got dressed up and a boy said she
   looked like a tart, or something.
★ Her pet dying.

If she found out her best friend
was going out with her boyfriend.

Do you think life is better for BOYS than for you?

❀ **IF BOYS HAD TO GIVE BIRTH THEY WOULD ALL ADOPT.**

❀ It's easier and more laid back for boys.

❀ Boys don't understand what girls have to go through – things like periods. If you say something or you're in a mood, they'll say, 'Uh-oh, someone's got PMT.'

❀ Boys are allowed to stay out longer, but if girls stay out, people think they're up to something. Girls get judged more than boys.

❀ Boys are more self-conscious when they're growing up and their voices break and they're all squeaky.

Do you think life is better for GIRLS than for you?

★ **GIRLS GET EVERYTHING THEY WANT.**

★ Girls have to go through having babies – morning sickness, the birth, etc.

Girls have a lot more friends than boys.

★ It's not as bad as things we have to deal with, like the embarrassment of wet dreams. Wet dreams are not considered natural, whereas periods are.

★ There's a lot more things they can do, like with their hair: they can put it in lots of different styles.

Would you like to be a BOY for just one day?

✿ **YOU'D GET TO KNOW THEIR SECRETS.**

✿ To see what they talk about with their mates.

✿ Yes. You could fix it so that a boy you fancy goes out with you.

✿ To get insight on what a boy's life is like.

✿ To see how differently they get treated.

✿ Yes, so you'd know how they'd feel when you were back to being a girl.

✿ To see which one's better.

✿ To see how easy it is to go up to a person and say, 'I think you're nice.'

✿ So I could be lazy for a day and not get told off.

✿ You'd get to see why lads are such jerks, why they've got to impress each other and why they have to be so hard.

Would you like to be a GIRL for just one day?

★ **YES: TO SEE HOW MANY LADS FANCY YOU.**

★ Yes: to hear the secrets.

★ Yes: to play with myself.

★ Yes: as a child, so I didn't have to have a baby.

★ Yes: you could wear lots of different clothes and their clothes are nicer than boys'.

★ Yes: to see what it was like to have big jugs!

★ Yes: to see what it's like to talk about everything.

★ To work out how they tick.
   To see what they're thinking.
   To understand what they mean.

★ Yes, so you won't get told off so much, because they're teacher's pets.

★ I'd try to remember what I would like as a girl when I come back as a boy.

★ Yes, so you can see yourself in the shower.

★ To promise someone to have a date with them and then you don't turn up.

★ No, it's too hard work.

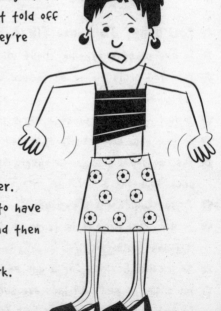

★ I'd like to experience how they can talk and write at the same time.
★ To go shopping!
★ I'd rather be a boy. I've seen all the acts. I'll give it a miss.

> If you were to come back in another life, would you like to come back as a BOY?

✿ **NO, BECAUSE BOYS ARE DISGUSTING!**
✿ Yes: they don't have to do their hair and they don't have to shave their legs. They don't have to wear bras either.
✿ Yes, because a boy's life doesn't seem as hard as a girl's – we've got to go through all the pain of things like labour and periods.
✿ I'd come back to be different to what the boys are towards me – I wouldn't take the mick when somebody falls over, I'd ask if they were all right. I'd be a nice boy. I'd be smart, I wouldn't be a bitchy boy.
✿ Yes, because we get all the pain, they get all the pleasure.
✿ I wouldn't, because women are stronger than men.
✿ No way. Boys have too much to live up to. If you're a boy and you're soft you get beaten up.
✿ No, I like being a girl better – you can have more fun!
✿ No, because you wouldn't get to go shopping.

If you were to come back in another life would you like to come back as a GIRL?

★ **I'D LIKE IT IF I WAS DEAD SEXY!**

★ No, because everything is worse off for them – having babies, cleaning, cooking.

★ No: they're the weaker sex.

★ Anything hurts them – they take things seriously, they can't take it as a joke.

★ No: because girls get more stressed out than boys.

★ No: I couldn't handle the pain of growing up, having periods, being pregnant, having babies and that.

★ No. they're too fussy. And there's all the housework – you'd be in the kitchen all the time.

★ Yes, so I could hear all the other girls' secrets.

★ Yes, for a different experience. I've done all the boy things, I could do the girl things.

★ Girls have more fun than boys: they have two parts of their body, boys have only one.

★ I wouldn't mind if I looked nice and had big breasts.

Thank you!

WE HOPE YOU ENJOYED READING THIS
BOOK AS MUCH AS WE ENJOYED
RESEARCHING AND WRITING IT.

OUR GRATEFUL THANKS GO TO THE
FOLLOWING PEOPLE:

✿

Anique Skinner and the Years Seven and Eight pupils
of Callington Community College, Callington, Cornwall.

★

Hamish Robertson, Andrew Robson and the
first-year pupils of Lasswade High School,
Bonnyrigg, Midlothian, Scotland.

✿

Jim O'Neill and the Year Eight pupils of Carmel
Technology College, Darlington.

★

Vivian Aldous and the Year Eight pupils of
Haberdashers' Aske's Hatcham College,
New Cross, London.

✿

Nigel Evans, Chris Fuell and the Year Seven pupils of
Clare Middle School, Sudbury, Suffolk.

★

Angela West, Pamela John and the Year Eight pupils
of Risca Community Comprehensive School,
Risca, South Wales.

❀

Alison Fawdrey and the Year Seven and Eight pupils
of Tividale High School and Community College,
Oldbury, West Bromwich.

★

Keith Hammond and the Year Seven pupils of
Bexleyheath School, Bexleyheath, Kent.

❀

Peter Earnshaw, Frank Havard, Alan Henderson and
the Year Nine pupils of the Hollins Technology
College, Accrington, Lancashire.

★

Pam Stevenson, Jeff Taylor, Lynne Craigs and the
Year Nine pupils of Hartshead High School,
Ashton-under-Lyne, Tameside.

❀

Jan Powling, at Speaking of Books.

★

Anne McNeil.

from

Anne Finnis ❖ Denis Bond

It's a girl thing!

Girls come round to comfort each other like a swarm of bees.

Girls are never apart from their bag.

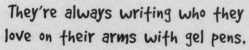

They're always writing who they love on their arms with gel pens.

Even if they only saw each other ten minutes ago they give each other a big hug.

If a boy dumps a girl – then all of his friends are on her hit-list.

Girls tell you off for everything you do.

It's a boy thing!

Boys always do their top tens. They'll put girls in a list of the best kissers or the best looking...

Boys always want the girls to know what type of boxers they're wearing. They have them hanging out of their trousers.

When boys are together they hit you and everything. But when they're on their own they're dead nice to you.

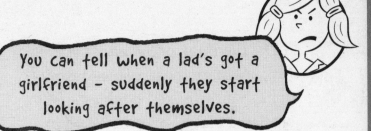

You can tell when a lad's got a girlfriend – suddenly they start looking after themselves.

It's the boys that have PMT, not us. They have constant PMT.

Boys don't think about what **YOU** want to do it's what **THEY** want to do.

Check out these summer sizzlers . . .

Temperatures and heart rates are rising in these red-hot reads . . .

In ***The Big Book of Summer Love*** the Brit babes face the sexy Swedes at tennis but the mixed doubles aren't just being played on court! And in ***The Big Book of Summer Snogs,*** can a coach load of fit footy fellas help Nia get over her dating disaster?

With saucy surfers and gorgeous Greek gods among the local attractions, these girls are in holiday heaven, but life's not always a beach when it comes to summer love . . .

Fun in the sun has never been so hot!

ISBN 0 09 940967 4

ISBN 0 09 941758 8

Win a year's free subscription to

Sugar

Enter our fab competition and you could bag yourself a year's free subscription to **Sugar**, Britain's best-selling girls' magazine, worth **£25.20**! It's your monthly fix of the hottest celebs, juiciest real life stories, funkiest fashion and the most embarrassing moments ever! Your prize subscription will also make sure the magazine is delivered straight to your door before it even hits the shops!

How to enter:

Simply log on to www.kidsatrandomhouse.co.uk /competition or send us a postcard with your name and address to:

Sugar competition (BoD),

Marketing Department, Random House Children's Books, 61-63 Uxbridge Road, London W5 5SA*

We will pick ten names at random on friday 25th April 2003. Each lucky winner will receive a year's subscription to **Sugar** magazine.

Terms and Conditions:

1. The winners will be the first ten names picked at random and will be notified by post or email.

2. The closing date for this prize draw is friday 25th April 2003. Entries received after this date will be ineligible. The draw will take pace on 28th April and the winners will be notified by 2nd May.

3. Entrants must be aged **13** or over.

4. The prize draw is open to residents of the UK and Republic of Ireland (excluding employees of The Random House Group Ltd, Sugar Magazine, Hachette Filipacchi UK Ltd and their families).

5. No cash alternative is available.

6. The judge's decision is final.

7. No correspondence will be entered into.

8. Only one entry per person.

9. No responsibility can be accepted for entries lost or damaged in the post.

10. No purchase is necessary.

* The Random House Group Ltd will process all personal data in compliance with the requirements of the Data Protection Act 1998. The Random House Group Ltd will not retain or use the personal data submitted for any purpose other than choosing and notifying winners in this prize draw, unless the entrant has specifically requested us to do otherwise.

www.kidsatrandomhouse.co.uk
www.sugarmagazine.co.uk